CLASSIC KITCHENS

BETA-PLUS

CLASSIC KITCHENS

January 2007
ISBN 13: 978 90 772 1366 7
ISBN 10: 90 772 1366 X

p. 2
An Obumex project.

p. 4-5
A Mape design.

CONTENTS

FOREWORD

In recent years, the kitchen has undergone a real metamorphosis.

This room has become one of the most important places in the home, providing space not only for cooking, but also for many other activities: eating, working, receiving guests...

The best multi-purpose kitchens effortlessly combine these many different facets, with designs by interior architects and kitchen designers that manage to transcend the purely utilitarian character of the kitchen.

A great deal of attention is paid to the ergonomics of the sink and cooking areas and to creating practical (often fully integrated) storage space, but the other aspects of the kitchen are just as important: a space to have breakfast or lunch, a place where the children can do their homework or simply somewhere to relax.

This completely new publication (2007-2008) features the most recent kitchen projects by leading interior specialists and kitchen designers. There is also a strong emphasis on high-quality kitchen equipment, including exclusive cookers, hobs and large refrigerators.

All of the kitchens in this book are designed in a timeless, country style. A companion title focusing on minimalist, modern kitchens is being published simultaneously: CONTEMPORARY KITCHENS.

Wim Pauwels
Publisher

A project by Il Etait Une Fois.

A Mape project.

PART I

INSPIRING PROJECTS BY LEADING KITCHEN DESIGNERS

OLD MATERIALS, CLEAN LINES

Architect Benoit Viaene renovated this distinctive house in close consultation with the client.

In this kitchen, old materials have been combined with clean, timeless lines.

The Devaere interior company was responsible for all of the construction work, masterfully translating the architect's vision and design to create this kitchen.

The cupboards are made of wide, vertical oak planks that have been brushed and stained.

Reclaimed white marble was selected for the floor.

An old chandelier has been given a new lease of life and integrated into this interior.

Old parquet has been reused to create this breakfast table.

Breakfast dresser in solid oak with sliding doors.

BENOIT VIAENE
Architectural studio
    Drabstraat 40
    B - 9000 GENT
    T +32 (0)9 330 65 56
    F +32 (0)9 330 65 56
    benoit.viaene@telenet.be

DEVAERE
Interiors
    Gentstraat 45-47
    B - 8780 OOSTROZEBEKE
    T +32 (0)51 40 05 96
    F +32 (0)51 40 59 22
    info@devaere-nv.be

Hand-finished natural stone was selected for the work surface.

An American side-by-side refrigerator and other kitchen equipment have been fully integrated into the wall unit.

THE ULTIMATE IN LUXURY

Clive Christian represents the ultimate in luxury and exclusivity in kitchens.
This English kitchen designer uses only the highest-quality materials (such as exquisite varieties of solid wood, rare natural stone and durable brass) that have been prepared by the best craftspeople to create real gems of skill and know-how.

The Antwerp interior-design company Amazing Interiors translates Clive Christian's kitchen and home-design philosophy to fit the context of the Low Countries: they design and coordinate the creation of these kitchens of worldwide renown for the most exacting customers in Belgium.

This Victorian kitchen in antique cream has been created according to artistic principles.
This arrangement contains all of the typical stylistic trademarks that make it so easy to recognise a Clive Christian kitchen.

A Staffordshire rack above the cooking island. Belgravia mantelpiece with a decorative feature and Belgravia pilasters around the island with its solid bluestone sink.

A brass tap with a "Quooker", or boiling-water tap, next to it.

An Aga in the Classic design.

Iroko wood surfaces and a specially selected Rose Aurore ultra clair natural stone.

All of the appliances have been expertly hidden away from view.
The washing-up area has a large fire-clay sink. The dishwasher is to the right
of the washing-up area and is built into the unit. A tile design by Lief Van
Himbeeck has been installed behind the Aga, as commissioned by the owners.
The wall units in the dining room consist of a butler's pantry flanked by display
cabinets with small wooden frames and faceted glass.

An Edwardian kitchen with a double row of wall cupboards, in ivory with additional patinated detail in the mouldings of the door panels. A classic kitchen, but with a contemporary atmosphere.

The incorporated symmetry is disrupted here and there, which creates a playful effect.

The blue walls give this kitchen a particularly fresh look.

A Lacanche cooker and a cooker hood with an external motor. Sink area with a mixer tap and a "Quooker".

Double ceramic sinks.

The American refrigerator has been clad with
furniture panels. The central unit has a Carrara
marble surface (with a 6cm-high contoured edge)
and is flanked by a chopping block in crosscut Iroko
wood and by a breakfast bar, also in Iroko wood. A
refrigerator and dishwasher have been incorporated
into the unit.

The kitchen continues on the other side, with
faceted-glass wall cupboards and a unit with built-in
kitchen appliances: an Imperial steamer and a
compact oven with a microwave function.

CLIVE CHRISTIAN BELGIUM

Amazing Interiors

    Leopoldsplaats 10

    B – 2000 Antwerp

    T +32 (0)3 226 71 45

    F +32 (0)3 232 34 59

    www.clive.com

    antwerp@clive.com

A PREFERRED PARTNER
FOR KITCHEN PROJECTS

Over thirty years, kitchen creator Liedssen has succeeded in building up a client base of over 9000 satisfied customers. This is quite a record of achievement for this company, which has always made quality and professionalism a top priority, supported by a team of enthusiastic and experienced staff.

All Liedssen kitchens, whether in a classic or contemporary style, are designed, created and installed according to the specifications and needs of the client.

Liedssen is the kitchen designer that many renowned architects and decorators prefer to use. Within three decades, the company has built up an outstanding reputation as a reliable partner for the creation of exclusive, durable kitchen projects.

Liedssen uses only high-quality varieties of wood and natural stone to create its custom-built kitchens.

LIEDSSEN

Wingepark 16
B – 3110 Rotselaar
T +32 (0)16 44 01 64
F +32 (0)16 44 01 80
www.liedssen.be
info@liedssen.be
Open Monday to Friday
from 10.00 to 12.00
and from 2.00 to 6.00.
Saturdays by appointment only.

KITCHEN DESIGN AND CREATION FROM A TO Z

Home Design provides a unique concept all under one roof: from kitchen design (by a team of experienced interior architects) to the construction and finishing, with a building contractor who takes care of every stage of the construction or renovation process: electricity, plumbing, carpentry, flooring, paintwork, and so on.

As well as kitchens, which are one of the specialities of Home Design, this Brussels company is also extremely skilled in creating and constructing exclusive bathrooms, dressing rooms, cloakrooms, right up to and including the complete coordination of a renovation project: from the structural work to the smallest details of the finish.

The Home Design showroom is available to help clients with the selection of materials, the presentation of furniture and lighting (Luz and XVL tables, Meridiani seating, S. Davidts lighting) and with inspiration for the creation of the complete interior.

This kitchen was custom built by Home Design and finished with Massangis work surfaces (Anciento finish with a contoured edge). The sink is in assembled Massangis.
The doors with panes of glass were painted by hand in the workshop with a matt varnish to ensure a better finish. The lighting is concealed behind the canopy moulding.

The cooker is by Smeg. Pendragon taps. The tiles on the wall are hand-made zeliges.

HOME DESIGN

avenue de Hinnisdael 14B
B – 1150 Brussels
T +32 (0)2 771 99 10
F +32 (0)2 770 78 85
www.homedesign .be
home.design@skynet.be

EXCLUSIVE KITCHENS TAILORED TO THE CLIENT'S NEEDS

Paul van de Kooi builds high-quality kitchens to correspond to the specifications and needs of his clients.

Whether it's a classic rustic-type kitchen or a more contemporary look, every project by Paul van de Kooi Kitchens is characterised by the constant pursuit of the very best standards through the exclusive use of high-quality materials that are handled by experienced professionals.

The kitchens presented in this report perfectly illustrate the skill of this renowned kitchen designer.
Clients are welcome to seek further inspiration in the company's showroom in Amersfoort, where there are always around fifteen exclusive kitchens on display.

Kitchen furniture in solid oak panels, with interiors in glued birch multiplex.

The Belgian bluestone work surface has a grooved finish along the front.

A Viking cooker, 122 cm wide.

A specially made wrought-iron rack for pots and pans above an original old butcher's block.

The solid oak panels have been finished with white Osmo. Nero Profondo granite was chosen as a work surface.

This tall wall unit has been "pushed" into the wall. An open scullery area.
Oven, steam oven, hot plate and deep-fryer by Gaggenau.

Eye-catching features in this kitchen are the large dresser and the 150cm-wide Lacanche cooker.

Belgian bluestone work surfaces, with a grooved finish along the front.

Solid oak spray-painted façades on the furniture. Interiors made of glued birch multiplex.

In the cooking area, the units follow the curve of the surface. The extractor chimney also curves in the same way.

The work surface of this kitchen was cast on-site in concrete.

Gaggenau kitchen equipment and a Sub Zero refrigerator, 122 cm wide.

An exclusive Paul van de Kooi kitchen with a Viking cooker in a restored farmhouse.

The 10cm-thick counter was seamlessly cast in concrete on-site (colour: anthracite) and two stainless-steel sinks were installed.

PAUL VAN DE KOOI

Heliumweg 40a
NL – 3812 RE Amersfoort
T +31 (0)33 465 11 11
F +31 (0)33 465 11 77
www.paulvandekooi.nl
info@paulvandekooi.nl

AN HONEST AND NATURAL PHILOSOPHY FOR LIVING

Frank Tack is the head of a third-generation family carpentry business, which has made a name for itself in recent years with its kitchens and complete projects in the typical Flemish country style.

Tack likes to use distinctive and honest materials: specially selected wood and hard-wearing, exclusive natural stone.

All of his kitchens are made to order with respect for the client's lifestyle. Creativity and symmetry are central to the design. The results are always suffused with a timeless, classic atmosphere.

Every project by Tack is studied in depth: the kitchen, table, chairs, interior doors, radiator boxes, wall treatments, advice on lighting and colours, and other elements are all considered.

The same high standards are applied when the company takes care of the complete outfitting of a house (dressing room, bathroom, library, and so on).

The bench is a Tack design, painted in harmony with the colour of the kitchen and the custom-made chairs and table.

The orangery behind was also designed and created by Tack.

The dresser has sliding doors at the
top and bottom.
The colour and lighting design
(both functional and atmospheric)
was also coordinated by Tack.

The double cupboard contains a
side-by-side fridge-freezer
combination.

p. 62

Taps in a pewter colour on a sink and work surface in exclusive solid aged bluestone with a contoured edge.

Symmetry has been imposed above and beside the wide Lacanche cooker: two display cabinets flank the cooker hood.

The Art Nouveau moulding matches the cooker hood.

Handles in authentic, aged tin. The dishwasher opens from the side.

A reserved, monastic atmosphere in this house designed by architect Stéphane Boens.

The kitchen concept is in keeping with the architecture of the building.

Doors with and without handles have been combined.

Vertical door panels in painted larch.

Work surfaces in white marble with an authentic serrated finish, 5 cm thick. The hatch by the cooking area opens by hand and provides a great deal of extra storage space.

A bottom-mounted refrigerator has been skilfully integrated into the cupboard units.

A Flemish retro kitchen style, with a solid bluestone sink and surface (5 cm thick).

In consultation with the client, a floor was selected to harmonise with the kitchen.

Different door designs in oak (using slats of wood and frames) have been combined and painted in a cream shade.

The wide extractor chimney above the Lacanche cooker and the tiles behind are reminiscent of the wide Flemish castle ovens of days gone by.

A dining area has been created beside the kitchen.

A perfect symmetry of doors and built-in dresser in this wall.

The solid oak doors have been painted in castle grey. The natural stone surface and vertical section harmonise with the floor. Above the Lacanche cooker is a large Flemish retro-style chimney. The classic moulding on the cupboards is repeated on the cooker hood.

TACK
Design and creation

> Grotstraat 74
> B – 8780 Oostrozebeke
> T +32 (0)51 40 47 18
> F +32 (0)51 40 61 40
>
> Menenstraat 472
> B – 8560 Wevelgem
> T +32 (0)56 42 50 95
>
> www.tack-keukens.be
> info@tack-keukens.be

THE KITCHEN AS THE CENTRAL ELEMENT OF A COMPLETE HOME-DESIGN CONCEPT

Country Cooking creates complete country-style interiors around the kitchen as the central unit, with old-fashioned craftsmanship (for example, mortise and tenon joints as a guarantee of quality), but also with a very modern outlook.

The company always employs high-quality solid materials: oak, pine and beech are used to create custom-built furniture, work surfaces for the kitchen are made with natural stone such as Spanish marble, and washbasins are in slate or authentic English porcelain.

This is the company philosophy and it is also a most successful concept for home design.

Country Cooking produces its own line of furniture, Doran, and its own range of colours.
These colours are reflected in the company's selection of paints, which lend a particular patina to the furniture, and also in the faience tiles on the rear walls of the kitchens, with integrated cookers from renowned companies such as the cast-iron Redfyre range cookers, Lacanche, Godin and Boretti.

This love for employing traditional methods to craft kitchens developed into a passion for creating complete interiors and pieces of furniture.
This passion then extended into finding the ideal accessories, such as floors, taps and tiles, to perfect these interiors.

p. 76-79

Composition of a solid pine kitchen, combined with an Italian Zucchetti tap and unglazed old-Dutch earthenware floor tiles.

The cast-iron Redfyre with its square lids and the double sink in solid bluestone complete this country kitchen.

The solid pine freestanding Lorraine dresser and the solid pine Fleur de Lys table with its oak top are part of the company's range of furniture.

This timeless kitchen has been finished in pale shades from the Whirling Dunes collection so as to accentuate the feeling of space.

The cast-iron Redfyre with its robust appearance and typical square hob lids is the beating heart of this kitchen, created by Country Cooking.

COUNTRY COOKING

Gerard Willemotlaan 104
B – 9030 Mariakerke (Gent)
T +32 (0)9 269 02 98
F +32 (0)9 269 03 01
www.countrycooking.be
info@countrycooking.be
Open on Thursday,
Friday and Saturday
from 10.00 to 1.00 and from 2.00 to 6.00.

TIMELESS KITCHEN DESIGNS

A passion for pure design, eye for detail and constant pursuit of perfection make De Menagerie one of the leading traditional kitchen designers in the Low Countries.

All of their designs are made to order and installed by the De Menagerie team.

Every project is unique and corresponds perfectly to the wishes of the client.

The concept is devised to be in harmony with the space, with functionality and aesthetics going hand in hand.

Both the rustic-style and the more contemporary kitchens created by De Menagerie are reduced to their essence, and are characterised by their timeless feel and warm atmosphere.

The extractor chimney above the Aga was specially constructed. Air is supplied through the vents on the splashback, which, like the work surfaces, is in Azul Valverde natural stone.
Kitchen furniture in solid oak with a patinated finish.
Floor in Cotto d'Este tiles.

The solid oak table was designed and created for this space.

Perrin & Rowe taps. Sink surrounds and surface clad in Azul Valverde.

Harmony in black (the Aga and the Moroccan zeliges) and burgundy (the walls and extractor chimney). The work surface and washing-up island are made from 5cm-thick French Massangis limestone with a smoothed finish and a contoured edge. The solid double sink unit is also carved from Massangis. The kitchen furniture is in solid patinated oak. Perrin & Rowe taps.
Oak plinth surround.

This cosy TV room provides a simple contrast. There are drawers without handles under the seating unit.

The wall with the open fireplace and the dining room were designed in collaboration with architect Bart De Beule. Wine alcoves and shelves in MDF with oak veneer.

A kitchen island built around the Viking cooker and Viking hood.

A heater has been incorporated into this central unit.

In the background, an Amana refrigerator, steam oven, microwave and a Miele wine cooler.

Silestone surface. The coffee machine, toaster and other kitchen equipment are handily concealed in two cupboards with roll-down shutters.

The tall cupboards and sink area are in lined, hand-painted MDF. DAL Ambiance lighting.

DE MENAGERIE

Leo de Bethunelaan 45
B – 9300 Aalst
T +32 (0)53 78 69 39
F +32 (0)53 70 79 96
www.demenagerie.be
info@demenagerie.be

p. 94
The wall behind the
sink is clad with
green zeliges.

A PASSION FOR
CUSTOM-MADE KITCHENS

Arcade Kitchens owes its enviable reputation to its custom-made kitchens and the turnkey concept.

Annick van der Wolf, the founder of Arcade, has always devised her exclusive kitchen designs with a great sense of creativity.

Arcade's construction of high-quality kitchens, which are entirely custom-made, is perfectly in keeping with the style of the classic "cottage" kitchen, but this company from Waals-Brabant also includes quite a number of contemporary designs on its list of achievements.

Arcade can even take care of the complete renovation and fitting-out of the kitchen space.

For this kitchen in a restored presbytery, interior architect Annick van der Wolf created a lived-in atmosphere: reclaimed terracotta "tomette" tiles, solid oak doors that have been oiled and polished white. The paintwork provides the finishing touch.

The kitchen work surface is in 5cm-thick smoothed bluestone with a grooved finish.

ARCADE

Avenue Comte d'Ursel 38

B - 1390 Grez-Doiceau (Wavre)

T +32 (0)10 84 15 05

F +32 (0)10 84 05 36

www.arcadecuisine.be

info@arcadecuisine.be

Open Monday to Friday from 1.30 to 6.00.

Saturday from 10.00 to 5.00 or by appointment.

Doors in raw, painted MDF. Kitchen surface in smoothed Zimbabwe natural stone. An open kitchen with a real atmosphere of warmth and cosiness.

RUSTIC INSPIRATION

Mape is a family concern that has specialised in the creation of kitchens and bathroom furniture for over forty years. The architecture, ergonomics and functionality of the kitchen are at the heart of every project: the kitchen is an essential element of the living environment.

All of the lacquering work is carried out in the company's own workshops and is of the highest quality.

The company's extensive kitchen range can be selected in different materials: from MDF with high-gloss or matt lacquer to solid natural or synthetic materials. All of the kitchens are developed by Mape's design team from the basic plan to create a unique design that corresponds perfectly to the wishes of the client.

This report presents two of Mape's kitchen creations that take their inspiration from the countryside.

The streamlined design and use of natural materials (oak and bluestone) give this kitchen an atmosphere of calm and simplicity.

Aged oak has been combined with an ancient monastery floor and a bluestone work surface.

The project was created in collaboration with architect Stéphane Boens.

The cupboards under the cooking island are without handles.

The MDF cooker-hood canopy has been painted in white lime paint.

The electrical equipment has been incorporated within the wall units, as have the cellar door and the double door into the living room.

Impressions of the scullery with its floor-to-ceiling cupboards, a washbasin in solid bluestone and Dornbracht taps.

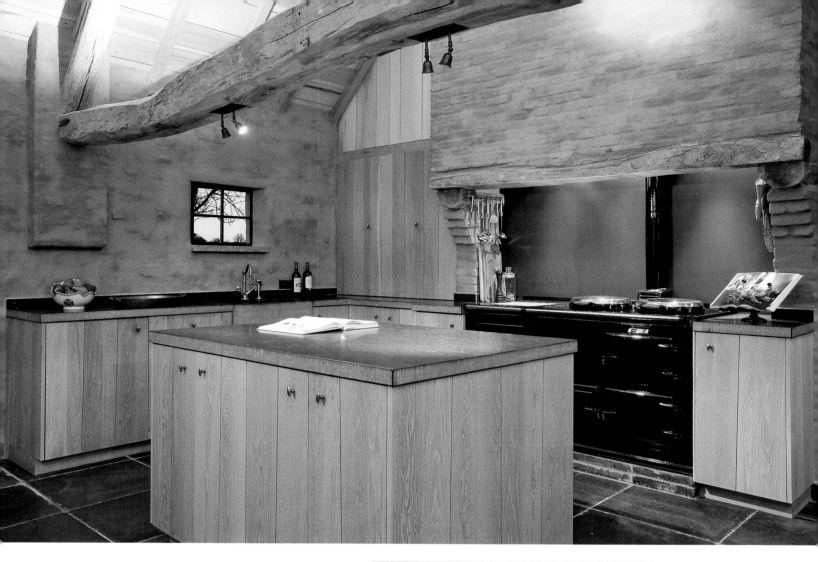

This cosy country kitchen has also been built in solid oak combined with bluestone. The oak beams are authentic and have been perfectly integrated into the design of this kitchen.

The extraction system has been concealed behind one of the existing solid oak beams.

An Aga range cooker. The cupboard on top of the work surface has been accommodated within the slope of the roof.

MAPE

Baardegemstraat 13
B – 9420 Erpe-Mere
T +32 (0)53 60 30 60
F +32 (0)53 63 09 23
www.mape.be
info@mape.be

A PASSION FOR PERFECTION IN DESIGN AND MATERIAL SELECTION

The De Keyzer family and their team have been passionate about techniques and interior design for over thirty years.

Driven by this passion, the company produces the highest-quality kitchens with simple and timeless designs, made with fine materials and with a desire for perfection that extends to even the smallest details.

Farm: the perfect symbiosis of warm nostalgia and timeless design.

The quality of top-grade oak has been combined with an exclusive lava stone.

This design has all the grandeur of an opulent castle kitchen.
The matching panelling, the authentic doors and the handcrafted dresser
complete the refined look.

DE KEYZER
Kitchen architecture
> Industrielaan 55
> B – 8930 Menen
> T +32 (0)56 52 13 40
> F +32 (0)56 52 13 41
> www.dekeyzer.be
> info@dekeyzer.be
>
> Shop Sint-Martens-Latem
> Kortrijksesteenweg 1
> B - 9830 Sint-Martens-Latem

THE POWER OF THREE

Art'Monia is a branch of L'Entrepôt de Verviers, which designs and creates custom-made kitchens.

Art'Monia's unique concept is its three-in-one set-up. The company houses a carpentry studio, a traditional painter's firm and a stonemason's workshop.

The carpentry studio employs only solid wood.
In the painting department, with its patina workshop, every detail of the kitchen design (existing floor, doors, colour of the walls) is studied in-depth so as to achieve perfect harmony. All of the paintwork is completed by hand.
Every project is designed and completed according to the needs and specifications of the client.

The individual approach comes first in the stonemason's workshop as well: clients are free to select their own stone and finish.

In addition to this, L'Entrepôt de Verviers also carries out complete interior design. Every one of the projects in this report has been created exclusively by this firm from Verviers, and designed, created and coordinated by company head Alain Degee.
Furniture, lighting, floors and decoration can all be entrusted to the company: a total solution tailored to the individual client and carried out from A to Z.

Art'Monia's traditional carpentry studio uses only solid wood.

The key word is harmony: all of the elements of the interior (colour, light, materials, and so on) have to tone perfectly.

In the stonemason's workshop, the client can select
the type of natural stone and the desired finish:
perhaps polished or smoothed or a different finish.
Art'Monia's patina workshop provides the finishing
touch: the samples are shown to the clients, whose
selection is then presented on oak to give an aged
look. After that, between four and eight hand-
applied layers are required to achieve the final result.

ART'MONIA
a branch of
L'ENTREPOT DE VERVIERS
> rue de Dinant 13-15
> B – 4800 Verviers
> T +32 (0)87 333 555
> F +32 (0)87 338 707
> lentrepot.verviers@skynet.be

DISTINCTIVE, DURABLE KITCHENS IN A TIMELESS ATMOSPHERE

Cousaert – Van der Donckt designs and creates complete interiors that are tailored to the client.

One of the specialities of this company from the Flemish Ardennes is the creation and construction of country kitchens. Traditional techniques are employed throughout: for example, joinery techniques such as mortise and tenon and tongue and groove are used, which have proved their efficiency and durability over the centuries.

This report presents some distinctive Cousaert – Van der Donckt kitchens that clearly illustrate the skill and the individual character of this traditional carpentry workshop.

A typical country kitchen, constructed with traditional methods according to the wishes of Cousaert – Van der Donckt's client. In the foreground is a spiral staircase with stairs made from an old oak beam. The terracotta floor tiles are from Cousaert – Van der Donckt.

In the background is a country-style iron cabinet based on an old model, finished with putty.

In the company showroom and workshops in Kluisbergen the visitor will always find a wide range of antique sinks (there are always around 150 in stock) that can be professionally installed into the custom-made kitchen furniture.

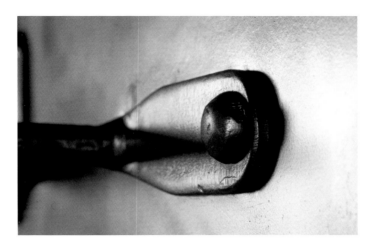

A passion for detail and respect for time-honoured traditional techniques.

p. 128

Cousaert – Van der Donckt has built a functional kitchen around the Lacanche cooker that radiates charm and authenticity. In the foreground, a section of the bluestone work surface, into which a sink has been cut. Grooved sides.

Impressions of an outside kitchen created by Cousaert – Van der Donckt, which can be admired at the Dutch garden and decorating centre Fattura Garden.

COUSAERT – VAN DER DONCKT
    Stationsstraat 160
    B – 9690 Kluisbergen
    T +32 (0)55 38 70 53
    F +32 (0)55 38 60 39
    www.cousaert-vanderdonckt.be
    www.keuken-cuisine.be
    info@cousaert-vanderdonckt.be
    Open Monday, Tuesday and Friday from 1.00 to 6.00.
    Saturday from 2.00 to 6.00 and
    last Sunday of the month from 2.00 to 6.00.

SOBER AND SERENE

Obumex shows its familiar signature, here in a classic style: a sober, serene living environment in which every moment of the day is a pleasure.

The living space and the cooking area flow seamlessly into each other. The word "kitchen" does not really apply here: this is clearly a living space par excellence, a real family room.

Cooking is the central element of this friendly, bustling space, where everyone can feel at home.

This sitting area filled with light combines with subtle colours and cosy seating in front of the TV to create a warm, inviting atmosphere.

OBUMEX

Showroom Staden
    Diksmuidestraat 121
    B - 8840 Staden
    T +32 (0)51 70 50 71
    F +32 (0)51 70 50 81
Showroom Antwerp
    L. de Waelplaats 20
    B - 2000 Antwerpen
    T +32 (0)3 238 00 30

Showroom Brussels
    Waterloolaan 30
    B - 1000 Brussels
    T +32 (0)2 502 97 80
Showroom Knokke
    Sparrendreef 83
    B - 8300 Knokke
    T +32 (0)50 601 666
    www.obumex.be
    design@obumex.be

EVERY KITCHEN TELLS A STORY

Anne De Visscher and her husband Eric Meert started designing and creating traditional kitchens in 1996.

Their company "Il Etait Une Fois" specialises in classic country kitchens with a timeless atmosphere.

All of their projects conform to the highest standards of quality: the kitchens are completely custom-made and adapted to the specifications of the client.
Upon installation, the furniture is painted by hand in harmony with the colour palette of the home.

Every kitchen tells a story, so Anne De Visscher and Eric Meert have given names to all of their designs: Cottage, le Nord, l'Ouest, le Sud, Romanoff. An example of each of these designs is featured in this report.

The Cottage design, with bluestone surfaces and a Cotto d'Este floor.
The furniture is in hand-painted hydrofuge MDF (colour: Rain Barrel).

A 140cm-wide Lacanche cooker (model: Sully) in "marron glacé" with teppan yaki and a warming plate.

The piece on the left of the photo was also created by Il Etait Une Fois (model: Tuileries). Ledge in white oiled oak.

In the foreground, a solid oak table.
Samuel Heath taps and a porcelain washbasin.

Le Nord: a kitchen style that fits perfectly in these converted stables. The kitchen furniture is painted in Langdon Dove; the walls are in Plymouth Beige. Smeg cooker and a Novy cooker hood. The General Electric refrigerator has been integrated into a unit. Kitchen surfaces in oiled oak with a contoured edge. Pendragon taps. Cotto d'Este ceramic-tile flooring (Buxy).

L'Ouest. The kitchen surface is in
smoothed bluestone with a contoured
edge. Pendragon taps; porcelain
washbasins and fittings.
Floor in Crema Marfil natural stone
with smoothed bluestone cabochons.

The Le Nord design. Above the Lacanche cooker (model: Vougeot), the wall has been clad with zeliges, mixed with cabochons in Agathe and Onyx. The furniture has been hand-painted in the Tarlatan shade. A wooden floor in aged oak.

The Romanoff design, with an ivory-coloured Lacanche
cooker (model: Cluny) and hand-painted kitchen
furniture (colour: Rain Barrel). Cotto d'Este floors.
White zeliges with inserts have been used again here.

Le Sud. Furniture painted in Rain Barrel here as well. Pendragon taps and a porcelain washbasin. Wooden blinds and a solid oak table, also produced by Il Etait Une Fois. Work surfaces in afrormosia wood.

IL ETAIT UNE FOIS ...

Place du Châtelain 10
B – 1050 Brussels
T +32 (0)2 537 07 05
F +32 (0)2 537 63 07
MOB +32 (0)475 787 133 (Anne De Visscher)
+32 (0)475 488 713 (Eric Meert)
+32 (0)476 50 44 21 (Catherine Mahieu)
www.iletaitunefois.be
iletaitunefois@skynet.be

Van Bunnenlaan 10
B – 8300 Knokke
Open on Saturdays, Sundays and holidays from 12.00 to 6.00.

TIMELESS AND ACTUAL

Simply designing a kitchen is not enough: the design has to be functional, aesthetically pleasing and distinctive into the bargain.
With over fifteen years of experience, interior architects Mr. and Mrs. Van Havere–de Hasque and their son Xavier design kitchens that perfectly fulfil all of these criteria.

The functional and practical aspects of the kitchen, the use of the space, the friendly atmosphere and the view are all of equal importance. At Ambiance Cuisine, good design is essential and has to respect the lifestyle and requirements of each individual client: washing and preparation areas, space for cooking and eating, storage... and a place where the whole family can come together.

The Ambiance Cuisine team takes care of not only the kitchen design, but also all of the work and installation. They recommend a contractor for every stage of the building or renovation process and then the company's fitters, with over twenty years of experience under their belts, get to work: they guarantee the smooth operation and perfect installation of your dream kitchen.

The quality of this classic kitchen lies in the perfect combination of a living space and a reception area. The seats/radiator grilles further underline the cosy atmosphere of this kitchen and dining area.

The multi-functional unit ensures that the two areas are in harmony. This central island has a number of functions, containing the dishwasher on the kitchen side and storage space on the side facing the dining area.

The crockery cupboards with the raised surface function both as a bar and as a serving area. This also keeps the sinks out of sight.

The cupboard doors are in hand-painted MDF. The interiors of the cupboards have been created with the same degree of attention and quality as the famous German brand Poggenpohl, for which Ambiance Cuisine is the Brussels distributor.

The Carlton tap is a chrome mixer unit from Hansgrohe's Allegra range. Miele steam oven and microwave and a 90cm Smeg oven. The Novy extractor has been integrated into an MDF unit (colour: Nepal).

AMBIANCE CUISINE
Chaussée de Waterloo 1138
B – 1180 Brussels
T +32 (0)2 375 24 36

AMBIANCE CUISINE
Avenue Reine Astrid 479-481
B – 1950 Kraainem
T +32 (0)2 767 12 17

www.ambiancecuisine.com

Open from Tuesday to Friday
from 10.00 to 1.00 and from 2.00 to 6.00.
Saturday from 10.00 to 6.00.

This custom-made kitchen has been built to incorporate a great deal of storage space in hand-painted MDF in shades of grey. This family kitchen is equipped with a bluestone work surface with a contoured edge.

The authentic character of this design can also be seen in the porcelain Villeroy and Boch washbasin and the Perrin & Rowe taps.

Above the Boretti cooker is a wall clad in white metro tiles. The knobs have a rusted finish.

The interior architects from Ambiance Cuisine work with the client from the concept stage, right through the floor-to-ceiling study to the selection of the smallest details, including the door furniture and the lighting.

CREATIVITY AND CRAFTMANSHIP

Fahrenheit is a kitchen designer and distributor of exclusive cookers and kitchen accessories. The company is based in Brussels and directed by Thierry Goffin, the founder of Fahrenheit.

All kitchens created by Fahrenheit exhibit the same attention to durability, selection of fine materials and perfect finish.

The two projects in this report perfectly demonstrate the company's passion for uncompromising quality.

In this former embassy, a magnificent manor house in Brussels, the clients wanted to double their kitchen space. This was made possible by integrating the covered terrace of the previous kitchen and demolishing a long wall.

In order to retain the manor-like character of the house, a Viking cooker was installed with an extractor chimney, opposite the central island where the meals are prepared. This island also serves as a U-shaped bar or table, where people can be invited round for informal and friendly dinners.

The shelving units are illuminated and have authentic blown-glass windows.

The furniture is in painted tulipwood. The work surfaces are in 4cm-thick black Zimbabwe granite, finished with a contoured edge.

The kitchen appliances are concealed behind the hatches.

The Dutch family living in this small castle on the leafy outskirts of Brussels had their dream castle kitchen designed and built by Fahrenheit.

The kitchen units, partly made in tulipwood, occupy almost all of the space up to the high ceiling. The 4cm-thick Carrara marble is finished with a contoured edge: this natural stone was selected for its classic appeal and beautiful lightness. The sink is cut from the same block as the work surfaces, creating a perfect sense of harmony. The old dumb-waiter has been restored and integrated into the custom-made furniture.

FAHRENHEIT

avenue Louise 130 b
B – 1050 Brussels
T +32 (0)2 644 28 00
F +32 (0)2 644 27 87
www.fahrenheit.be
fahrenheit@fahrenheit.be

PART II

EXCLUSIVE MATERIALS AND KITCHEN WARE

NEW ÉLAN

The family concern Louis Culot bvba has for three generations been the natural-stone supplier of choice for many kitchen designers and private clients who want a new kitchen.

The significant growth within the company that Louis Culot and his team have experienced in recent years prompted them to seek a new base where there would be more space for the offices, showroom and workshops. At the beginning of 2007, the company relocated to the Pullaar industrial zone in Puurs.

The speciality of Louis Culot bvba is the custom cutting and finishing of natural stone for use in the kitchen. The company uses high-technology, computer-controlled CNC machines to produce perfectly finished kitchen surfaces within a short period of time.

The professional approach, competitive prices, outstanding service and the quality of the finish are just some of the selling points of this dynamic family company.

p. 162-165
The tops in this kitchen and the wall behind the Lacanche cooker are all made of Belgian bluestone.

LOUIS CULOT

Natural-stone suppliers

    Industriezone Pullaar

    Schoonmansveld 7

    B – 2870 Puurs

    T +32 (0)3 860 70 70

    F +32 (0)3 860 70 79

    www.culot.be

    info@culot.be

PERFECTION DOWN
TO THE SMALLEST DETAIL

Dauby nv has developed a considerable reputation over the past 20 years as the leading importer of exclusive door furniture in the Benelux countries.

The company specialises in quality door fittings that lend style and charm to any interior, whatever the style of construction: new-build homes, renovations of country houses, manors, presbyteries and modern townhouses.

The emphasis is on traditionally produced accessories for doors and furniture, window and security fittings and countless other features.

The showroom is very popular with architects, interior designers, restaurateurs, and others for whom quality, right down to the smallest detail, is of the utmost importance.

Anyone looking for high-quality items to lend a finishing touch to their home should make an appointment with Dauby. They have a huge assortment to please everyone and the team of interior designers is on hand to help if required.

This iron door opens stylishly with the old, traditionally crafted Genifer door handle, in harmony with the silver Giara fittings that were also finished by hand and cast in sand moulds.

Created by: Poppels Meubelhuis.

The highest quality in the kitchen itself as well, thanks to the use of old and top-grade materials by Giara and Genifer.

Created by: Poppels Meubelhuis.

Giara has an exceptional collection that was created after extensive research into different styles of architectural design over the years. These origins stretch far back into the Middle Ages. The material used here is Britannium metal, which fits perfectly with natural materials such as marble (Belgian red marble in this case) and bluestone. Created by: Poppels Meubelhuis.

The forms are pure, timeless, beautifully designed, conform to modern-day environmental standards and are all created according to time-honoured traditions of craftsmanship.

Created by: Poppels Meubelhuis.

Genifer is a traditional product that embellishes the kitchen and the rest of the home. All of the handles can also be supplied in a tilt-and-turn version. The entire Genifer range has been created in the spirit of old designs and can be used to form a theme that runs throughout the home.
Created by: Van Opstal.

One of the versions of the familiar railway handle, "chemin de fer". Here it is being used as a furniture knob. This range can be extended to doors and windows throughout both the interior and exterior of the home and is available in many different finishes and materials.
Created by: Van Opstal.

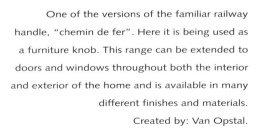

The Giara handles on this dresser look just like jewels and create a truly stylish interior.

The knobs have been cast in bronze and naturally oxidised.

Created by: Van Opstal.

DAUBY nv
Offices and store
      Uilenbaan 86
      B-2160 Wommelgem
      T +32 (0)3 354.16.86
      F +32 (0)3.354.16.32
      www.dauby.be
      info@dauby.be
      Open Monday to Thursday
      from 8.30 to 5.30.
      Friday from 8.30 to 5.00.

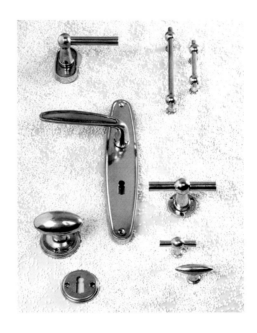

This window handle is also available as a door handle.

Created by: Van Opstal.

HIGH-END COOKERS
AND KITCHEN WARE

The Ghent company Adek was founded in 1980 and within a quarter of a century has become one of the leading distributors of top-quality cookers and other kitchen equipment in the Benelux countries.

Adek displays and supplies cookers from major manufacturers such as Delaubrac, Viking, Esse, Morice, Lacanche, Mercury, Cucineria, Smeg, Rosières, Metal Industries Lyon, La Cornue and others.

For customers who are looking for powerful, but quiet extractor systems, Adek usually suggests a custom-made cooker hood. Different types of motor can be combined with built-in systems and pullout cooker hoods or decorative extractor chimneys.

The company's range of exclusive refrigerators and storage units is also impressive, including models by Sub Zero, Norcool, Amana, Festivo, Liebherr, Eurocave, Müller, U-Line, General Electric and Smeg.

Finally, Adek also supplies built-in appliances for the kitchen, selecting only the very best for their showroom: Gaggenau, Küppersbusch, Miele, Imperial, Neff, Siemens, Mercury, Novy, Kitchenaid, Fisher & Paykel, Magimix, Lavazza, Bamix – a most varied selection with one common factor: the absolute top quality and exclusivity of every make.

At Adek there are unusual cookers and appliances that can be found in only very few places. It is most definitely worth paying a visit to the showroom in Sint-Amandsberg (near Ghent).

An all-electric Esse cooker with four ovens in a house designed by architect Bernard De Clerck.

This kitchen and dining area was designed by architect Bernard Van Eecke (Arcas Group and Pencil & Paper), who opted for features including a Mercury cooker and a fully integrated bottom mount refrigerator.

An Esse cooker: an extremely sound and robust piece, ideal for the classic country kitchen.

Delaubrac Champenois 120 with two electric ovens, four open fires and a "coupe-feu".

ADEK

Grondwetlaan 81
B – 9040 Gent (Sint-Amandsberg)
T +32 (0)9 251 49 99
F +32 (0)9 251 65 64
Showroom opening hours: Tuesday to Friday from 1.00 to 6.00.
Saturday from 10.00 to 12.00 and 1.30 to 5.00.

www.adek.be
info@adek.be

A Delaubrac cooker Provençal, 160 cm, in black.
A Costermans kitchen project.

GREAT CLASSICS

For over a quarter of a century, Alfa Belgium has been the exclusive importer of the legendary Aga cookers in Belgium and Luxembourg.

The Aga was invented in 1922 by the Swedish physicist and Nobel Prize winner Dr. Gustaf Dalén. He designed a cooker that was thermostatically controlled and very safe. It is the only cooker that is made completely from refined cast iron. Nowadays, Aga cookers are produced in England, where there are still very large foundries.

Some time ago, the company also became the exclusive distributor for Falcon in Belgium and Luxembourg.

The first Falcon cooker was made in 1833. Five generations of experts have made this cooker into a bestseller. In 2007, Alfa Belgium/Alfa Bis is placing the focus on three Falcon designs: the "Classic Deluxe", the "Excel" and the "Deluxe CT".

Alfa Belgium also won the right in 2004 to import the top-quality French La Cornue cookers into Belgium: this was a new development for this family company from Ghent, which within twenty-five years has become the port of call for advice on all three top-quality brands of cooker.

p. 188-189
Interior architect Annick Colle designed this kitchen in a country home with an Aga (a 4-oven gas-fired model with a black finish).

A 4-oven oil-fired Aga in an interior project by Lefèvre Interiors.

A Château 150 cooker by La Cornue in stainless steel and enamel with a satinised nickel/stainless-steel finish.
Created by Themenos.

A Château 120 in black enamel, in a project by Walda Pairon.

A Falcon Deluxe 1092.

ALFA BELGIUM nv / ALFA BIS bvba
 Showroom:
 Nijverheidskaai 2
 B – 9040 Gent
 T +32 (0)9 228 14 84
 F +32 (0)9 228 06 13
 www.aga.be
 info@aga.be
 www.falconkookfornuizen.be
 www.lacornue.fr

THE FINISHING TOUCH

Lerou was founded in 1792 and so is one of the oldest Belgian companies specialising in door and window furniture, restoration and security fittings and exclusive kitchen, bathroom and cloakroom accessories, inside and outside lighting, taps and other features.

The emphasis is on exclusive, traditionally produced restoration fittings: the company is very popular with architects, interior specialists, restorers and cabinetmakers who set great store by traditional craftsmanship. Private individuals are also welcome at Lerou.

Iron shell-shaped and olive-shaped handles are often used in the country kitchen.

A solid brass tap and an iron olive-shaped
knob for the window.

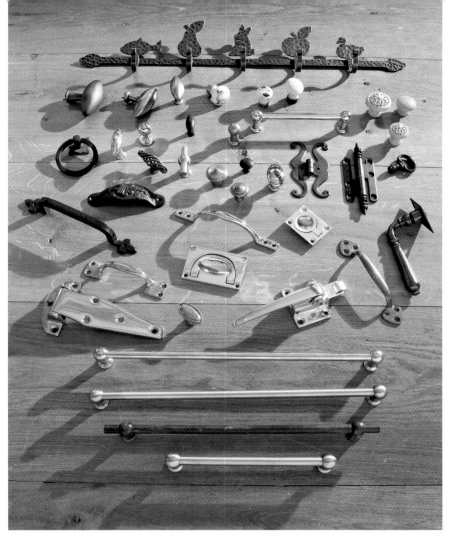

A small sample of the selection of kitchen fittings available from Lerou.

Lerou Ijzerwaren nv

Monnikenwerve 131
Industriezone Blauwe Toren
B – 8000 Bruges
T +32 (0)50 31 74 42
F +32 (0)50 31 01 60
www.lerou.com
info@lerou.com
Opening hours:
Monday to Friday
from 8.30 to 12.00
and from 1.30 to 6.00.
Saturday from 9.00 to 12.00.
Home visits by appointment.

Hand-crafted copper sinks.

LACANCHE COOKERS: COLOURFUL RENEWAL

Abel Falisse has for many years been the exclusive Belgian importer of Lacanche cookers.

Lacanche is a village in Burgundy, which has lent its name to one of the finest cookers for the classic and contemporary kitchen.

The history of Lacanche has, since the nineteenth century, been inextricably linked to its foundry, which increasingly focused on the production of cookers and kitchen equipment.
Lacanche's "pianos gastronomiques" are based directly on the cookers used by professional chefs and their top-quality features deliver outstanding results.

All Lacanche cookers are made to order, in a variety of sizes and models, and with a unique range of colours, from white, ivory and almond, to Delft, Portuguese and French blue, terracotta and chestnut, black, Sologne green – the choice is vast.

Many interior architects, kitchen designers and enthusiastic cooks have already placed their trust in Lacanche, as is demonstrated by the number of Lacanche cookers in this book and the colourful Lacanche models in this report.

One of the new Lacanche colours is chestnut ("marron glacé"), used here for the 2-oven Cluny model.

Lacanche offers a wide range of models and colours. This is only an impression of the selection: on the left-hand page is a Chambertin cooker in chestnut; above, a Chagny mandarin, Chassagne stainless steel, Cluny Delft blue, Vougeot Burgundy red, Sully frangipane and Fontenay Provence yellow.

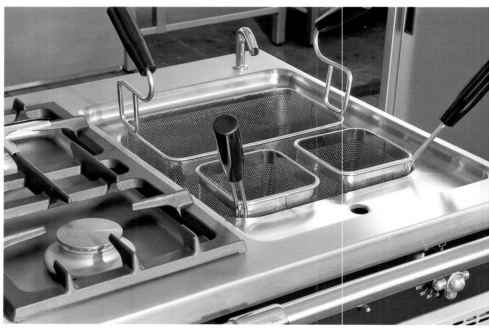

Depending on the model selected, customers can choose their own configuration of the cooking, grilling and frying sections. Below left, the famous "salamander" electric roasting spit.

Below right, a multi-cooker with three functions: steaming, bain-marie or cooking pasta (see photo above).

150cm-wide Fontenay model in English green.

A Cîteaux model in Delft blue, with two ovens of different sizes and a warming compartment.

Ets. ABEL FALISSE nv

    (Exclusive importer)

    T +32 (0)4 252 71 73

    F +32 (0)4 252 12 79

    www.lacanche.be

    info@abel-falisse.be

    (Showroom in Brussels

    by appointment)

A 180cm-wide Cluny cooker with a cooker hood in French blue.

ADDRESSES

Ets. ABEL FALISSE sa
(Exclusive importer)
T +32 (0)4 252 71 73
F +32 (0)4 252 12 79
www.lacanche.be
Info@abel-falisse.be
(Showroom Bruxelles by appointment
p. 198-203

ADEK
Grondwetlaan 81
B – 9040 Gent (Sint-Amandsberg)
T +32 (0)9 251 49 99
F +32 (0)9 251 65 64
Opening hours showroom:
Tuesday to Friday from 1 to 6.
Saturday from 10 to 12 and 1.30 to 5.
www.adek.be
info@adek.be
P. 180-185

ALFA BELGIUM / ALFA BIS
Showroom:
Nijverheidskaai 2
B – 9040 Gent
T +32 (0)9 228 14 84
F +32 (0)9 228 06 13
www.aga.be
info@aga.be
www.falconkookfornuizen.be
www.lacornue.fr
p. 186-191

AMBIANCE CUISINE
Chaussée de Waterloo 1138
B – 1180 Brussels
T +32 (0)2 375 24 36
AMBIANCE CUISINE
Avenue Reine Astrid 479-481

B – 1950 Kraainem
T +32 (0)2 767 12 17
www.ambiancecuisine.com
Open Tuesday to Friday
from 10 to 1 and 2 to 6.
Saturday from 10 to 6.
P. 150-155

ARCADE
Avenue Comte d'Ursel 38
B - 1390 Grez-Doiceau (Wavre)
T +32 (0)10 84 15 05
F +32 (0)10 84 05 36
www.arcadecuisine.be
info@arcadecuisine.be
Open Monday to Friday from 1.30 to 6.
Saturday from 10 to 5
and by appointment.
p. 96-101

ART'MONIA
division of
L'ENTREPOT DE VERVIERS
rue de Dinant 13-15
B – 4800 Verviers
T +32 (0)87 333 555
F +32 (0)87 338 707
lentrepot.verviers@skynet.be
p. 116-123

CLIVE CHRISTIAN BELGIUM
Amazing Interiors sprl
Leopoldsplaats 10
B – 2000 Antwerpen
T +32 (0)3 226 71 45
F +32 (0)3 232 34 59
www.clive.com
antwerp@clive.com
p. 24-33

COUNTRY COOKING sprl
Gerard Willemotlaan 104
B – 9030 Mariakerke (Gent)
T +32 (0)9 269 02 98
www.countrycooking.be
Open Thursday, Friday and Saturday
from 10 to 1 and to 6.
p. 76-83

COUSAERT – VAN DER DONCKT
Stationsstraat 160
B – 9690 Kluisbergen
T +32 (0)55 38 70 53
F +32 (0)55 38 60 39
www.cousaert-vanderdonckt.be
www.keuken-cuisine.be
info@cousaert-vanderdonckt.be
Open on Monday, Tuesday and Friday
from 1 to 6.
Saturday from 2 to 6 and last Saturday
of the month 2 to 6.
p. 124-131

CULOT LOUIS sprl
Natural-stone supplier
Industriezone Pullaar
Schoonmansveld 7
B – 2870 Puurs
T +32 (0)3 860 70 70
www.culot.be
info@culot.be
P. 166-169

DAUBY sa
Offices and warehouse
Uilenbaan 86
B-2160 Wommelgem
T +32 (0)3 354.16.86
F +32 (0)3.354.16.32
Open Monday to Thursday from 8.30 to 5.30.
On Friday from 8.30 to 5.
p. 170-179

DE KEYZER
Kitchen Architecture
Industrielaan 55
B – 8930 Menen
T +32 (0)56 52 13 40

F +32 (0)56 52 13 41
www.dekeyzer.be
info@dekeyzer.be
Shop Sint-Martens-Latem
Kortrijksesteenweg 1
B – 9830 Sint-Martens-Latem
p. 110-115

DE MENAGERIE
Leo de Bethunelaan 45
B – 9300 Alost
T +32 (0)53 78 69 39
F +32 (0)53 70 79 96
www.demenagerie.be
info@demenagerie.be
p. 84-95

DEVAERE sa
Interiors
Gentstraat 45-47
B - 8780 OOSTROZEBEKE
T +32 (0)51 40 05 96
F +32 (0)51 40 59 22
info@devaere-nv.be
p. 16-23

FAHRENHEIT
Avenue Louise 130 b
B – 1050 Brussels
T +32 (0)2 644 28 00
F +32 (0)2 644 27 87
www.fahrenheit.be
fahrenheit@fahrenheit.be
P. 156-163

HOME DESIGN
avenue de Hinnisdael 14B
B – 1150 Woluwe St. Pierre
T +32 (0)2 771 99 10
F +32 (0)2 770 78 85
www.homedesign .be
home.design@skynet.be
p. 40-43

IL ETAIT UNE FOIS ...
Place du Châtelain 10
B – 1050 Brussels
T +32 (0)2 537 07 05

F +32 (0)2 537 63 07
MOB +32 (0)475 787 133 (Anne De Visscher)
+32 (0)475 488 713 (Eric Meert)
+32 (0)476 50 44 21 (Catherine Mahieu)
www.iletaitunefois.be
iletaitunefois@skynet.be
p. 138-149

LEROU IJZERWAREN nv
Monnikenwerve 131
Industriezone Blauwe Toren
B – 8000 Brugge
T +32 (0)50 31 74 42
F +32 (0)50 31 01 60
www.lerou.com
info@lerou.com
Opening hours:
Monday to Friday from 8.30 to 12.00
and from 1.30 to 6.00.
Saturday from 9.00 to 12.00.
Home visits by appointment.
p. 192-197

LIEDSSEN
Wingepark 16
B – 3110 Rotselaar
T +32 (0)16 44 01 64
F +32 (0)16 44 01 80
www.liedssen.be
info@liedssen.be
Open Monday to Friday
from 10 to 12 and 2 to 6.
Saturday only by appointment.
p. 34-39

MAPE sa
Baardegemstraat 13
B – 9420 Erpe-Mere
T +32 (0)53 60 30 60
F +32 (0)53 63 09 23
www.mape .be
info@mape.be
p. 102-109

OBUMEX
Showroom Staden
Diksmuidestraat 121
B - 8840 Staden

T +32 (0)51 70 50 71
F +32 (0)51 70 50 81
Showroom Anvers
L. de Waelplaats 20
B - 2000 Anvers
T +32 (0)3 238 00 30
Showroom Brussels
Bd. de Waterloo 30
B - 1000 Brussels
T +32 (0)2 502 97 80
Showroom Knokke
Sparrendreef 83
B - 8300 Knokke
T +32 (0)50 601 666
www.obumex.be
design@obumex.be
p. 132-137

TACK
Concept and production
Grotstraat 74
B – 8780 Oostrozebeke
T +32 (0)51 40 47 18
F +32 (0)51 40 61 40
Menenstraat 472
B – 8560 Wevelgem
T +32 (0)56 42 50 95
www.tack-keukens.be
info@tack-keukens.be
p. 60-75

PAUL VAN DE KOOI KITCHENS
Heliumweg 40a
NL – 3812 RE Amersfoort
T +31 (0)33 465 11 11
F +31 (0)33 465 11 77
www.paulvandekooi.nl
info@paulvandekooi.nl
p. 44-59

VIAENE BENOIT
Architect
Drabstraat 40
B - 9000 GENT
T +32 (0)9 330 65 56
F +32 (0)9 330 65 56
benoit.viaene@telenet.be
p. 16-23

PUBLISHER

BETA-PLUS Publishing

Termuninck 3

B - 7850 Enghien (Belgium)

T +32 (0)2 395 90 20

F +32 (0)2 395 90 21

www.betaplus.com

betaplus@skynet.be

PHOTOGRAPHY

All pictures: Jo Pauwels, except for p. 38-39: Serge Anton

p. 124-131 Moniek Peers

GRAPHIC DESIGN

POLYDEM

Nathalie Binart

TRANSLATION

Laura Watkinson

January 2007

ISBN 13: 978 90 772 1366 7

ISBN 10: 90 772 1366 X